Great Tastes
of MICHIGAN

Written by Dianne Glupker

Watercolors by Dawna Delsi

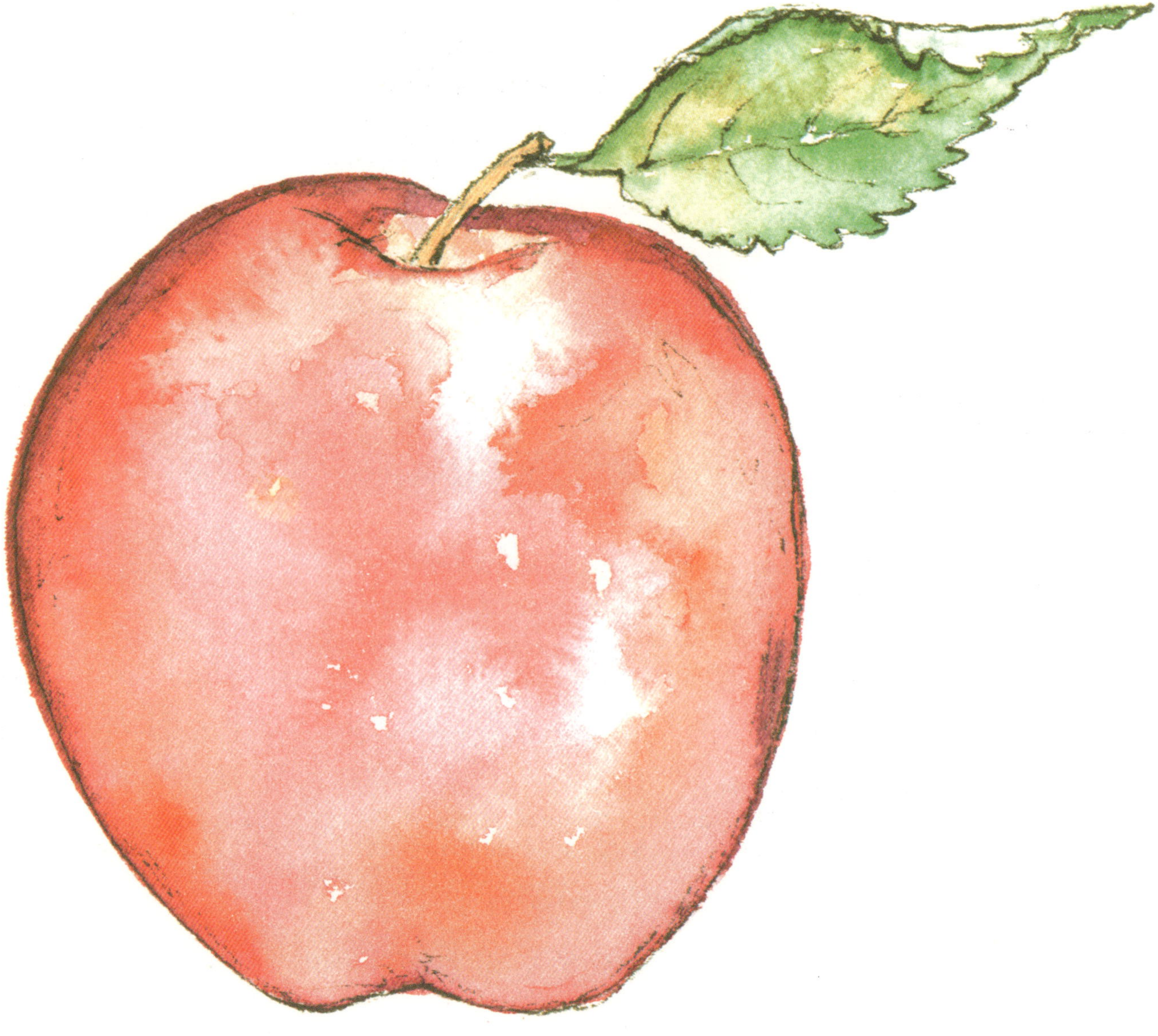

Published by
Harambee Press

P.O. Box 353
Macatawa, MI 49434
www.harambeepress.com

Text copyright 2007 by Dianne Glupker
Illustrations copyright 2007 by Dawna Delsi

All rights reserved. No part of this book may be reproduced or transmitted in any form or any means, electronic or mechanical; including photocopying, recording or any information storage or retrieval system, without permission from Harambee Press.

Library of Congress Control Number: 2006929611

Glupker, Dianne
　Great Tastes of Michigan/Dianne Glupker
　Illustrated by Dawna Delsi
p.　　cm.
　　Summary: A selection of twelve Michigan food festivals.
　　Descriptions include festival locations, history of selected foods and recipes.

1. Education/Travel   2. Michigan food festivals-Juvenile Non-Fiction   3. Cooking

ISBN: 978-0-9769846-1-0
The text of this book is set in 14 point Georgia.
Illustrations are watercolor paintings reproduced in full color.

Cover by DZ'ign Art

Printed in MICHIGAN, USA

They say the way to a man's heart is through his stomach.
I dedicate this book to the four men in my life,
my husband Curt and three sons, Chad, Chris and Ben.
dlg

To my husband, John.
I love you a bushel and a peck
and a hug around the neck.
dd

Dear Reader,

    Numerous cities in Michigan, both large and small, host food festivals. We give you a sampling of these festivals in our book.

    Good nutrition is important for a healthy lifestyle. Nutritious meals begin with nutritious ingredients. Michigan grows fruits and vegetables needed to get the necessary vitamins and minerals in your diet.

    We've tried to include healthy recipes that appeal to young people. We strongly recommend adult supervision while making these recipes.

                                      Happy reading and bon appetit!

        Harambee (pronounced ha-RAMH-beh), a Swahili word, is the national motto of Kenya.
                                        It means cooperation in community.
                          Kenyans have a strong desire to help one another, as do we.

                 We wish to extend this spirit of giving by donating a portion
                      of our book's proceeds to MICHIGAN food pantries.

TABLE OF CONTENTS

National Cherry Festival - Traverse City.. p 8

National Asparagus Festival - Oceana County... p 10

Peach Festivals - Coloma, Romeo, Elberta.. p 12

National Strawberry Festival in Belleville, other festivals in Chassell and Hartford............... p 14

Corn Festivals - Auburn, Corunna... p 16

Mint Festival - St. Johns... p 18

Pumpkin Festivals - Zeeland, Romulus, South Lyon, Caro.. p 20

Melon Festival - Howell... p 22

Potato Festivals - Posen, Munger, Elmira... p 24

National Blueberry Festival in South Haven, others in Imlay City, Montrose, Paradise........ p 26

National Pickle Festival in Linwood, Christmas Pickle Festival in Berrien Springs/Eau Claire p 28

Apple Festivals - Charlevoix, Charlotte... p 30

Answer Key.. p 32

GLOSSARY

ferment: to boil
herb: any plant used as a medicine or flavoring
moderate: mild
perennial: grows year after year
prune: to cut away unnecessary parts, to improve production, improve shape
salt brine: water heavily saturated with salt solution
scurvy: a disease characterized by body weakness and soft gums
tubular: shaped like a tube
versatile: can be used in many different ways

WEIGHTS AND MEASUREMENTS

3 teaspoons = 1 tablespoon = 1/2 fluid ounce
4 tablespoons = 1/4 cup = 2 fluid ounces
8 tablespoons = 1/2 cup = 4 fluid ounces
12 tablespoons = 3/4 cup = 6 fluid ounces
16 tablespoons = 1 cup = 8 fluid ounces

2 cups = 16 fluid ounces = 1 pint
4 cups = 32 fluid ounces = 1 quart
4 quarts = 1 gallon
8 quarts = 1 peck
4 pecks = 1 bushel

NATIONAL CHERRY FESTIVAL
Traverse City - July

Beautiful cherry blossoms in the spring give way
to the National Cherry Festival held each year in Traverse City.
The Grand Traverse area, in northwest Michigan, is ideal for growing cherries.
In fact, it has approximately 2 million tart cherry trees.
Sandy soil and Lake Michigan are two important factors for growing cherries.
The soil allows for good drainage. In addition, Lake Michigan offers cool breezes
in summer and moderate air temperatures in the winter.
Michigan produces 70-75% of the tart cherries in our country.
The cherries are used for jellies, juices, dried fruit,
pies and preserves.

Math Moment

The average number of tart cherries on one tree is 7000.
It takes about 250 cherries to make 1 pie.
Each tree could produce enough cherries for how many pies?

CHERRY SALSA

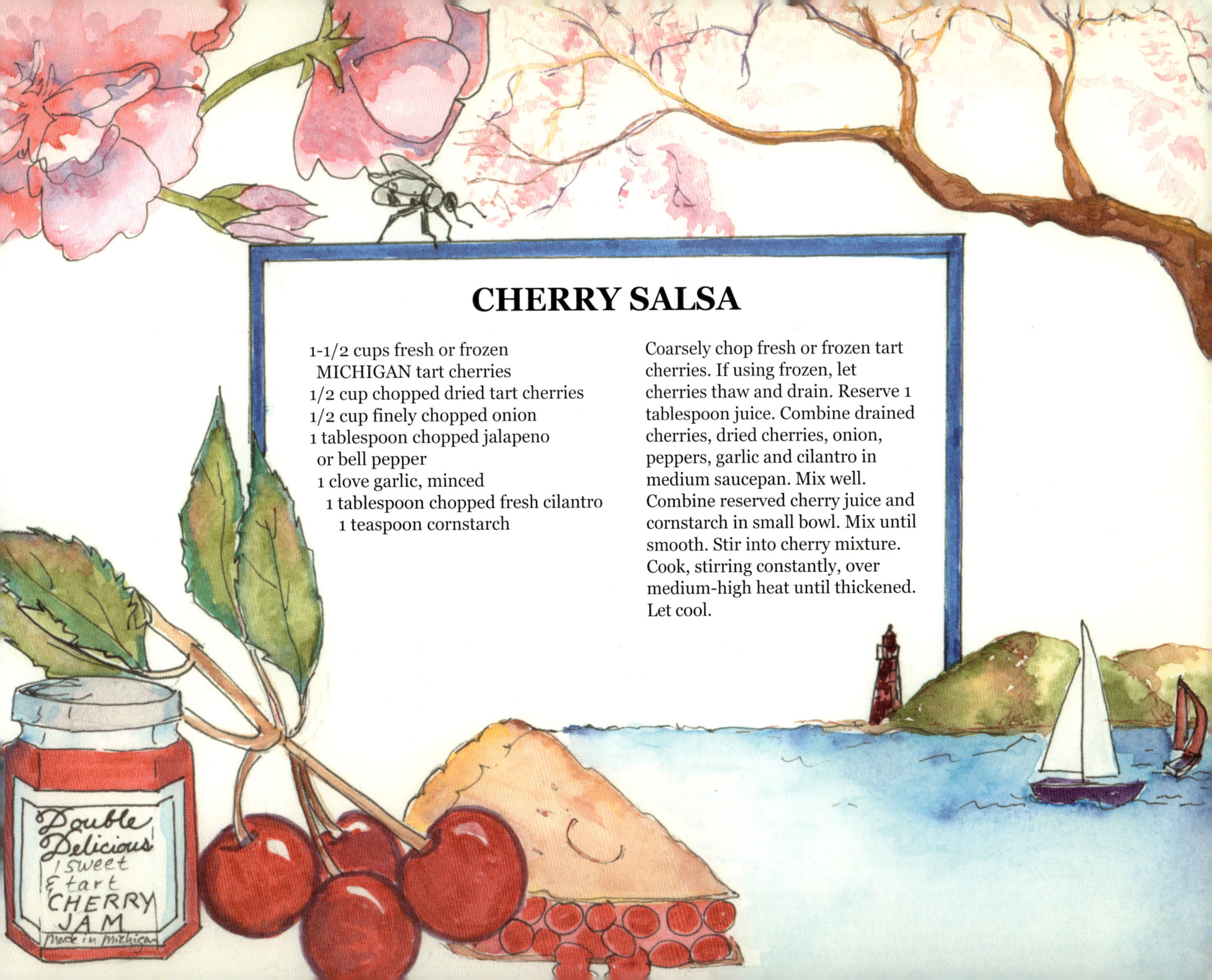

1-1/2 cups fresh or frozen MICHIGAN tart cherries
1/2 cup chopped dried tart cherries
1/2 cup finely chopped onion
1 tablespoon chopped jalapeno or bell pepper
1 clove garlic, minced
1 tablespoon chopped fresh cilantro
1 teaspoon cornstarch

Coarsely chop fresh or frozen tart cherries. If using frozen, let cherries thaw and drain. Reserve 1 tablespoon juice. Combine drained cherries, dried cherries, onion, peppers, garlic and cilantro in medium saucepan. Mix well. Combine reserved cherry juice and cornstarch in small bowl. Mix until smooth. Stir into cherry mixture. Cook, stirring constantly, over medium-high heat until thickened. Let cool.

NATIONAL ASPARAGUS FESTIVAL
Oceana County - June

The towns of Hart and Shelby alternate hosting the National Asparagus Festival.
Oceana County, near Lake Michigan, is our country's third largest producer of asparagus.
This nutritious, green vegetable was known to grow in Greece 2500 years ago.
It is part of the lily family and the Greek word means stalk or shoot.
Greeks believed asparagus had medicinal powers such as curing toothaches.
Oceana County provides well-drained, sandy soil needed to grow this crop.
An asparagus plant starts out as a tiny, black seed.
One year after planting, the seed turns into a long, **tubular** root called a crown.
The crown develops 6 inches of root and forms into a fern in the second year.
Finally, in the third season, the asparagus is ready for harvest.
Asparagus can grow up to 10 inches in a day.

Math Moment

After 6-8 years asparagus plants will yield 1-2 tons per acre.
How many pounds is equal to 1 ton?

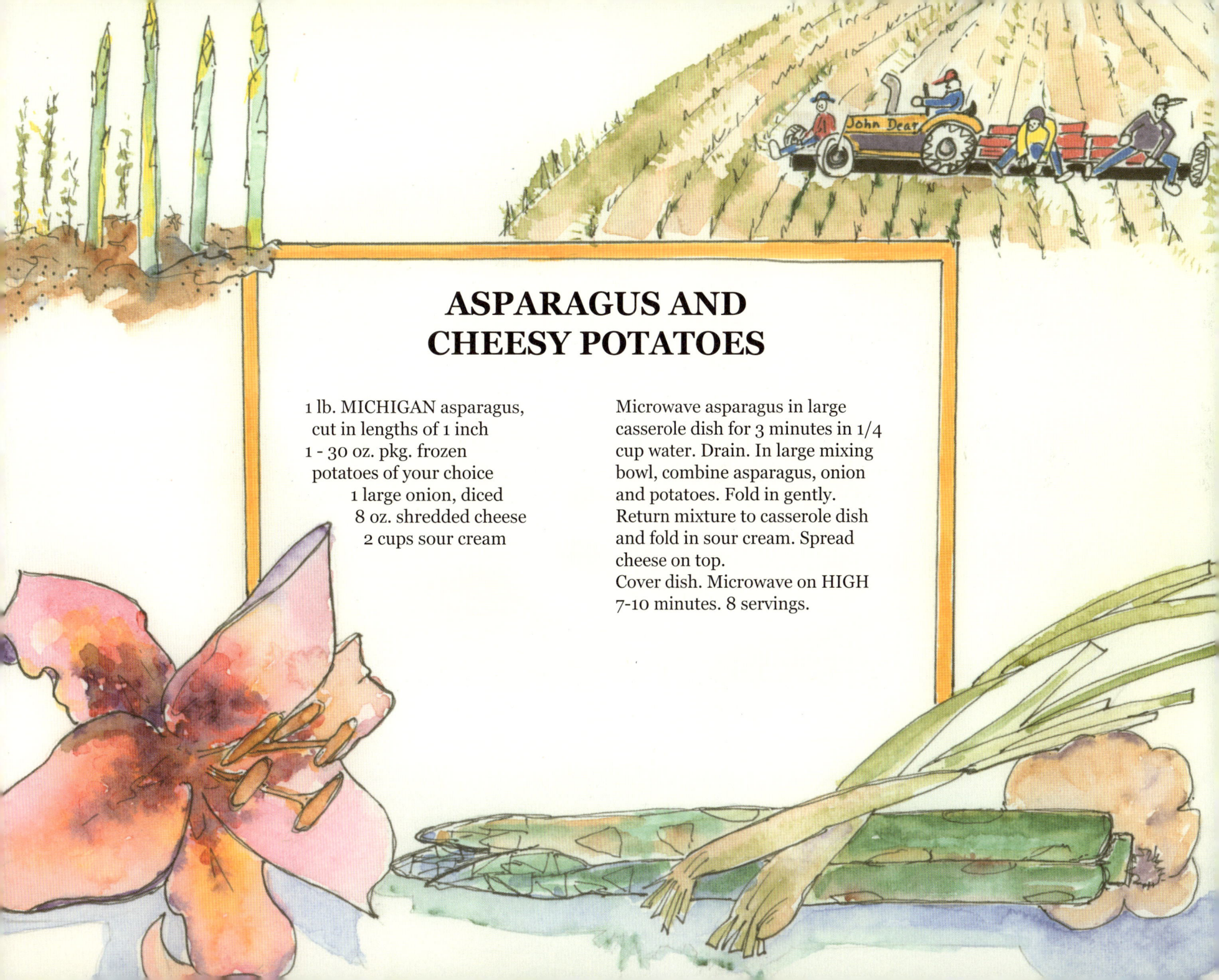

ASPARAGUS AND CHEESY POTATOES

1 lb. MICHIGAN asparagus, cut in lengths of 1 inch
1 - 30 oz. pkg. frozen potatoes of your choice
1 large onion, diced
8 oz. shredded cheese
2 cups sour cream

Microwave asparagus in large casserole dish for 3 minutes in 1/4 cup water. Drain. In large mixing bowl, combine asparagus, onion and potatoes. Fold in gently. Return mixture to casserole dish and fold in sour cream. Spread cheese on top.
Cover dish. Microwave on HIGH 7-10 minutes. 8 servings.

PEACH FESTIVAL
Coloma - August

Coloma is in the southwest part of our state, close to Lake Michigan.
China is said to be the place where peach trees first grew.
The Chinese considered peaches a symbol of longevity and good luck.
Peach trees were first planted in Michigan in the 1780's and
Michigan ranks 6th in our country in production.
Most of the largest peach farms are along the western shore
of Lake Michigan. The lake's cool breezes in summer and
moderate temperatures in winter help keep the trees healthy.
The fall is the best season to plant peach trees. It usually takes
about three years for the trees to produce fruit.
In addition, peach trees should be **pruned** every year.
Romeo, a city north of Detroit, holds a peach festival every year
and the town of Elberta, in northwest Michigan, hosts an annual peach festival.

Math Moment

The average peach tree grows to about 18 feet tall.
How many inches are in 18 feet?

PEACH SMOOTHIE

1 cup low-fat peach yogurt
3/4 cup peach nectar
1/2 cup fresh raspberries, frozen
1-1/2 cups fresh MICHIGAN peaches, diced and frozen

Place yogurt and nectar in blender. Add frozen raspberries and peaches. Blend until smooth
2 servings

NATIONAL STRAWBERRY FESTIVAL
Belleville - June

This annual festival is held in the southeastern part of Michigan.
The strawberry is thought to have grown in ancient Roman times.
Romans served strawberries at important events.
It was thought eating this food led to peace and prosperity.
Later, in our country, Native Americans taught colonists
how to crush the fruit to make a cornmeal bread.
The colonists created their own version and called it "strawberry shortcake."
The strawberry is the only fruit bearing seeds on the outside.
It grows in any type of soil but does best in cool, moist climates.
It is also the first fruit ready for picking in the spring.
Other Michigan cities hosting strawberry festivals are
Chassell in the upper peninsula and Hartford in southwest Michigan.

Math Moment

1 1/2 pounds of strawberries equal 2 pints or 1 quart.
How many pounds do you need to make 8 quarts?

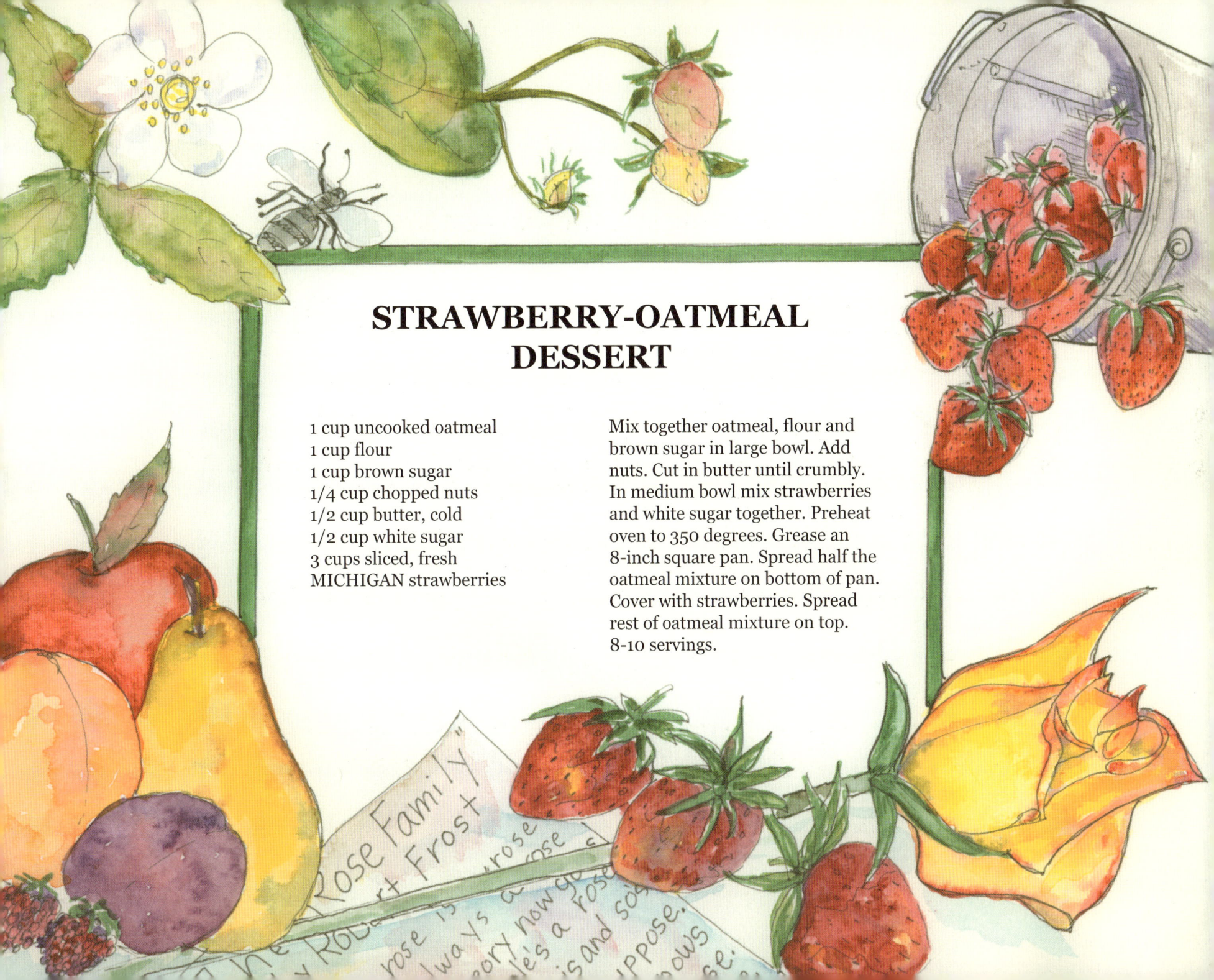

STRAWBERRY-OATMEAL DESSERT

1 cup uncooked oatmeal
1 cup flour
1 cup brown sugar
1/4 cup chopped nuts
1/2 cup butter, cold
1/2 cup white sugar
3 cups sliced, fresh MICHIGAN strawberries

Mix together oatmeal, flour and brown sugar in large bowl. Add nuts. Cut in butter until crumbly. In medium bowl mix strawberries and white sugar together. Preheat oven to 350 degrees. Grease an 8-inch square pan. Spread half the oatmeal mixture on bottom of pan. Cover with strawberries. Spread rest of oatmeal mixture on top. 8-10 servings.

CORN FESTIVAL
Auburn - July

Auburn, near the thumb area of Michigan, hosts a corn festival every year. Corn is America's number one field crop. The production of corn is double that of any other crop grown in our country. Michigan is the 6th largest producer. Corn is thought to have developed in Central Mexico some 7000 years ago.
The four most common types of corn are:
Flint corn: This is commonly known as Indian corn with its colorful kernels.
Dent corn: This is field corn used to feed livestock.
Sweet corn: This corn is eaten at our dinner tables. It is called "sweet" corn because it contains more sugar than the other types of corn.
Popcorn: This is a favorite snack food for many.
In fact, the average American consumes about 68 quarts of popcorn each year.
Corunna, a city east of Flint, is also host to an annual corn festival.

Math Moment

An average ear of corn holds approximately 800 kernels.
A family of four each eating 2 ears of corn
would consume how many kernels of corn?

GRILLED CORN ON THE COB

Fresh ears of corn, husked
Butter spray
Lime
Chili powder

In large pot of boiling water, cook corn 3-4 minutes. Remove corn. Spray with butter. Place corn on hot barbecue grill. Cook until grill marks appear and corn is re-heated. Remove and squeeze lime juice over corn. Sprinkle with chili powder and salt, if desired.

MINT FESTIVAL
St. Johns - July

St. Johns is a city north of Lansing, our state capital.
It is home to the annual Mint Festival.
Spearmint and peppermint plants are **herbs** and are grown in St. Johns.
Both of these fragrant herb plants were first used by Greeks and Romans
for flavoring food and as a medicine.
English colonists brought these **perennial** plants to America.
The plants grow to about 2-3 feet in height. The best time to
harvest them for oil is when they are beginning to flower.
Once the plants are cut and chopped, the oil is separated from the leaves.
Long periods of sunlight are needed in order to produce large amounts of oil.
Mint is used for flavoring gum, toothpaste, mouthwash, candy and medicine.
One pound of oil is enough to flavor 135,000 sticks of gum.

Math Moment

St. Johns is approximately 25 miles north of Lansing.
If you travel by car at 50 miles per hour,
how long will it take you to drive from St. Johns to our capital city?

MINT CHOCOLATE-CHIP COW

1/2 cup chocolate syrup
1/2 pint Hudsonville* chocolate-chip mint ice cream
1/4 teaspoon mint extract
1-1/2 cups cold milk

Mix chocolate syrup, ice cream, mint extract and milk in a blender. Beat until smooth.
Optional: Garnish with fresh mint.

* Hudsonville ice cream is made in Holland, our home town.

PUMPKIN FESTIVAL
Zeeland - October

Zeeland is a city in western Michigan near Holland, our home town.
They celebrate the harvest season with an annual Pumpkin Fest.
Pumpkin is a Greek word "pepon" which means large melon.
They have grown in North America for about 5000 years.
In our country, Native Americans used the seeds for food and medicine.
Today, the pumpkin is also used for animal feed.
Did you ever wonder how the early colonists baked pumpkin pie
for the first Thanksgiving feast?
They sliced off the tops of the pumpkins and removed the seeds.
Next, they filled the pumpkin shells with milk, spices and honey.
Then, they baked the filled pumpkins over hot ashes.
Some other Michigan cities hosting pumpkin festivals are
Romulus and South Lyon, in the Detroit area and Caro, in the thumb area.

Math Moment

You and a friend scoop out seeds from a pumpkin.
You count out 276 seeds.
How many dozen seeds did you count?

PUMPKIN SOUP

4 tablespoons butter
1 med onion, finely chopped
2 carrots finely chopped
2 cans (14 oz. ea.) chicken broth
1 cup water
1 can (29 oz.) solid-pack pumpkin
1 MICHIGAN golden delicious apple, cored and chopped
1 teaspoon ground ginger
1 teaspoon salt
1/4 teaspoon ground nutmeg
1 cup heavy cream

Melt butter in large saucepan over med-high heat. Add onion and carrots. Cook 5 minutes. Add broth, water, pumpkin, apple, ginger, salt and nutmeg. Bring to boil. Reduce heat to med-low. Simmer 30 minutes stirring occasionally. Cool slightly. Puree in batches in blender. Return to pan. Whisk in cream. Reheat, but do not boil.

MELON FESTIVAL
Howell - August

Howell, about halfway between Lansing and Detroit, holds a melon festival in the summer.
Melons were first grown in the Middle East and this sweet fruit spread to Europe.
It is thought that Christopher Columbus brought melon seeds
to the New World on his second voyage in 1494.
The melon is a member of the gourd family, same as squash.
Melons and squashes are similar because they both have
thick, outer flesh and their middles are filled with seeds.
Melons grow best in sunny locations and need a lot of space to grow on the vine.
It takes approximately 85-100 days for melon seeds to produce fruit.
Michigan produces a round, sweet melon called muskmelon or honeyrock melon.
Choosing a ripe melon can be tricky. Gently press your thumb on the stem.
If it gives a little, the melon is ready to eat.

Math Moment

If it takes approximately 100 days for melon seeds to produce fruit,
how many weeks would that be?

MELON-CUCUMBER CHICKEN SALAD

3 cups chicken, cooked, cut up
1 cup melon, cut up
1 cup cucumber, cut up
1 cup red, seedless grapes
1 cup slivered almonds
2/3 cup mayonnaise
2 teaspoons grated lime zest

Mix all ingredients in large bowl. Chill 2 hours before serving.
6 servings.

POTATO FESTIVAL
Posen - September

Posen is in northeast Michigan, close to Lake Huron.
They host a potato festival every year.
Potatoes were first grown by the Inca Indians of Peru around 200 BC.
They were grown for food but also for medicinal purposes.
The Incas believed placing raw slices of this vegetable
on broken bones would help in the healing process.
Michigan is 10th in the nation for potato production but it
continues to be our state's largest vegetable crop.
The round, white potato is grown in Michigan and this variety
is used for making potato chips, a popular snack food.
Three-quarters of Michigan's potato crop is used for potato chips.
Other cities hosting potato festivals are Munger, in the thumb area
and Elmira in northwest Michigan.

Math Moment

The average American eats approximately 124 pounds of potatoes per year.
How many pounds do they eat per week?

WHITE ROASTED MICHIGAN POTATOES

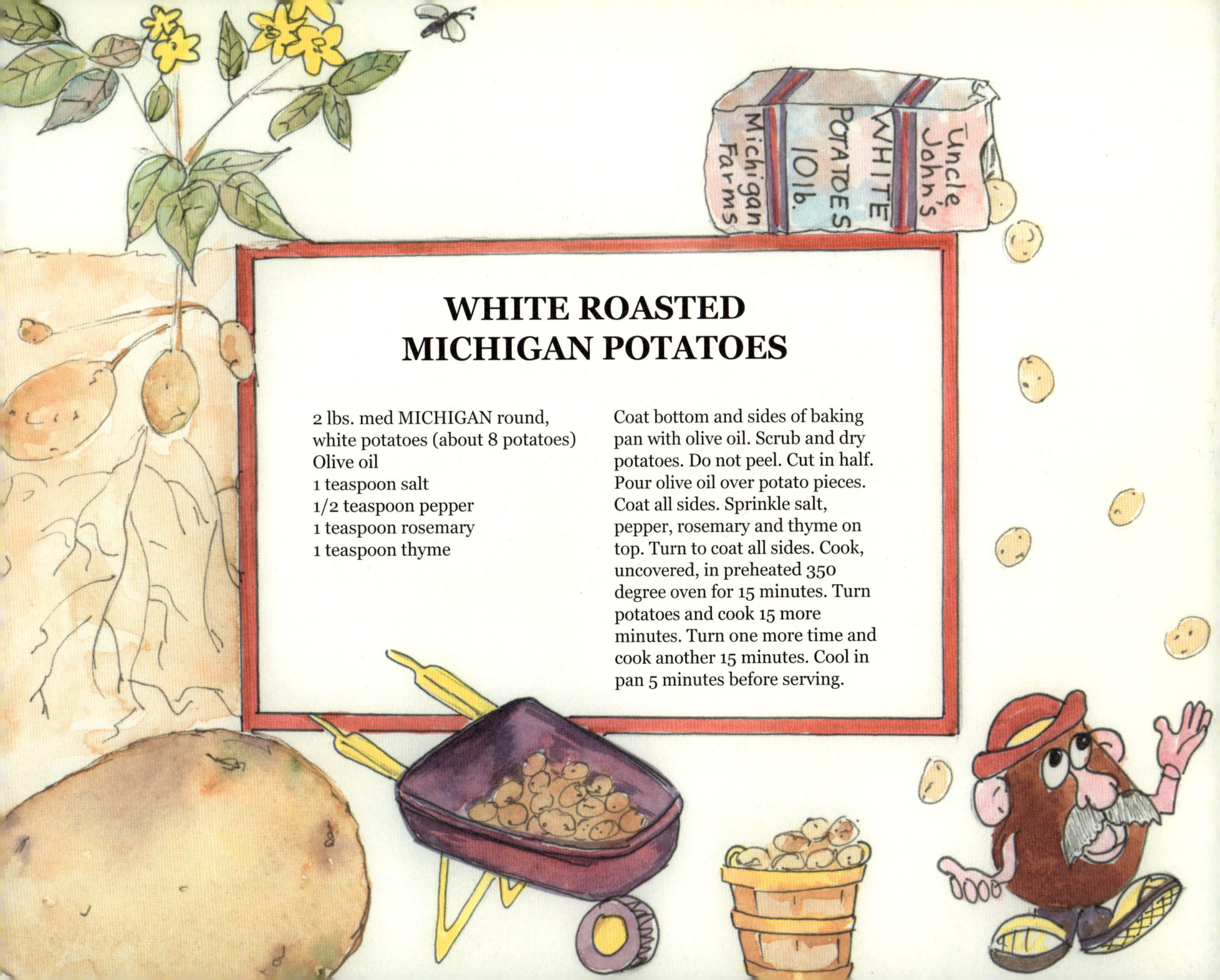

2 lbs. med MICHIGAN round, white potatoes (about 8 potatoes)
Olive oil
1 teaspoon salt
1/2 teaspoon pepper
1 teaspoon rosemary
1 teaspoon thyme

Coat bottom and sides of baking pan with olive oil. Scrub and dry potatoes. Do not peel. Cut in half. Pour olive oil over potato pieces. Coat all sides. Sprinkle salt, pepper, rosemary and thyme on top. Turn to coat all sides. Cook, uncovered, in preheated 350 degree oven for 15 minutes. Turn potatoes and cook 15 more minutes. Turn one more time and cook another 15 minutes. Cool in pan 5 minutes before serving.

NATIONAL BLUEBERRY FESTIVAL
South Haven - August

This southwest Michigan city is home to the National Blueberry Festival.
Blueberries are not only one of the few fruits that are truly blue in color,
they are also one of the few fruits native to North America.
In fact, the Indians called the blueberry "star fruit."
If you look at the blossom end of each berry
you will notice it takes the shape of a perfect 5-point star.
The Indians taught the Pilgrims how to gather and dry blueberries
in the sun in order to preserve them for winter.
Other Michigan cities hosting blueberry festivals are
Imlay City and Montrose, in the lower peninsula,
and Paradise in the upper peninsula.

Math Moment

The South Haven area produces blueberries from a variety of bush called "highbush."
Approximately 1200 bushes are planted per acre.
How many bushes would a farmer plant on a 25 acre farm?

MICHIGAN BLUEBERRY PANCAKES

1 cup all-bran cereal
1 egg, slightly beaten
1-1/4 cups buttermilk
2 tablespoons cooking oil
1 cup all-purpose flour
1 tablespoon sugar
1 teaspoon baking powder
1/2 teaspoon baking soda
1/2 teaspoon salt
1/2 cup fresh MICHIGAN blueberries

Crush cereal in blender or food processor. Stir together egg, buttermilk, oil, and cereal in medium bowl. Let stand for 7 minutes. Beat in flour, sugar, baking soda, baking powder and salt with a wire whisk or fork until blended. Gently stir in blueberries. Pour 1/4 cup batter onto hot griddle. Cook pancakes until puffed and full of bubbles. Turn and cook other side until golden brown.

makes 10 (5 inch) pancakes.

NATIONAL PICKLE FESTIVAL
Linwood - August

Linwood is a city near Saginaw Bay, in the eastern part of Michigan,
and it hosts the National Pickle Festival every summer.
Pickles were first eaten and preserved 4500 years ago in the region of Mesopotamia.
Americans have enjoyed their taste since the arrival of the Nina, Pinta and Santa Maria.
Pickles are rich in vitamin C. For that reason, they were brought over on ships
to help prevent the spread of **scurvy** among the sailors.
Then, during WWII, the armed forces received 40% of the country's pickle production.
All pickles start out as cucumbers. Our country has many cucumber pickle factories,
including one in our home town of Holland.
These factories usually **ferment** cucumbers in large outdoor vats filled with **salt brine.**
Pickles are fat-free and low in calories. The average dill pickle has only 15 calories.
Pickles can be used to add flavor to salsas, sauces, sandwiches, soups, appetizers and main dishes.
A Christmas Pickle Festival is also held every year in the Berrien Springs/Eau Claire area.

Math Moment

If the average dill pickle has 15 calories and a jar holds 2 dozen,
how many calories does the jar hold in all?

DILL PICKLE ROLL-UPS

24 dill pickles
1/2 pound deli ham slices
8 oz. cream cheese, softened
Dill weed
Chives
Celery seed

Drain pickles well. Spread cream cheese on ham slices. Sprinkle with dill weed, chives and celery seed, to taste. Wrap pickles with cream cheese filled ham slices. Makes 24 appetizers.

APPLE FESTIVAL
Charlevoix - October

An apple festival is held each fall in this northwest Michigan city.
Apples are a member of the rose family and actually grew
in the Middle East more than 4000 years ago.
Overall, Michigan ranks third in apple production in our country.
Michigan ranks first in production of Jonathan and Northern Spy apples.
Red and golden delicious apples are also a large part of production.
Apples are so **versatile** that they can be baked, fried, dried, and
squeezed to make applesauce and cider.
Do you know the reason why we can bob for apples?
Fresh apples float because 25% of their volume is air.
The apple blossom was adopted as Michigan's state flower in 1897.
Charlotte, in the south central part of Michigan, also holds an apple festival.

Math Moment

It takes the juice of approximately 36 apples to make 1 gallon of cider.
How many apples are needed to make a dozen gallons?

EASY CARAMEL APPLES

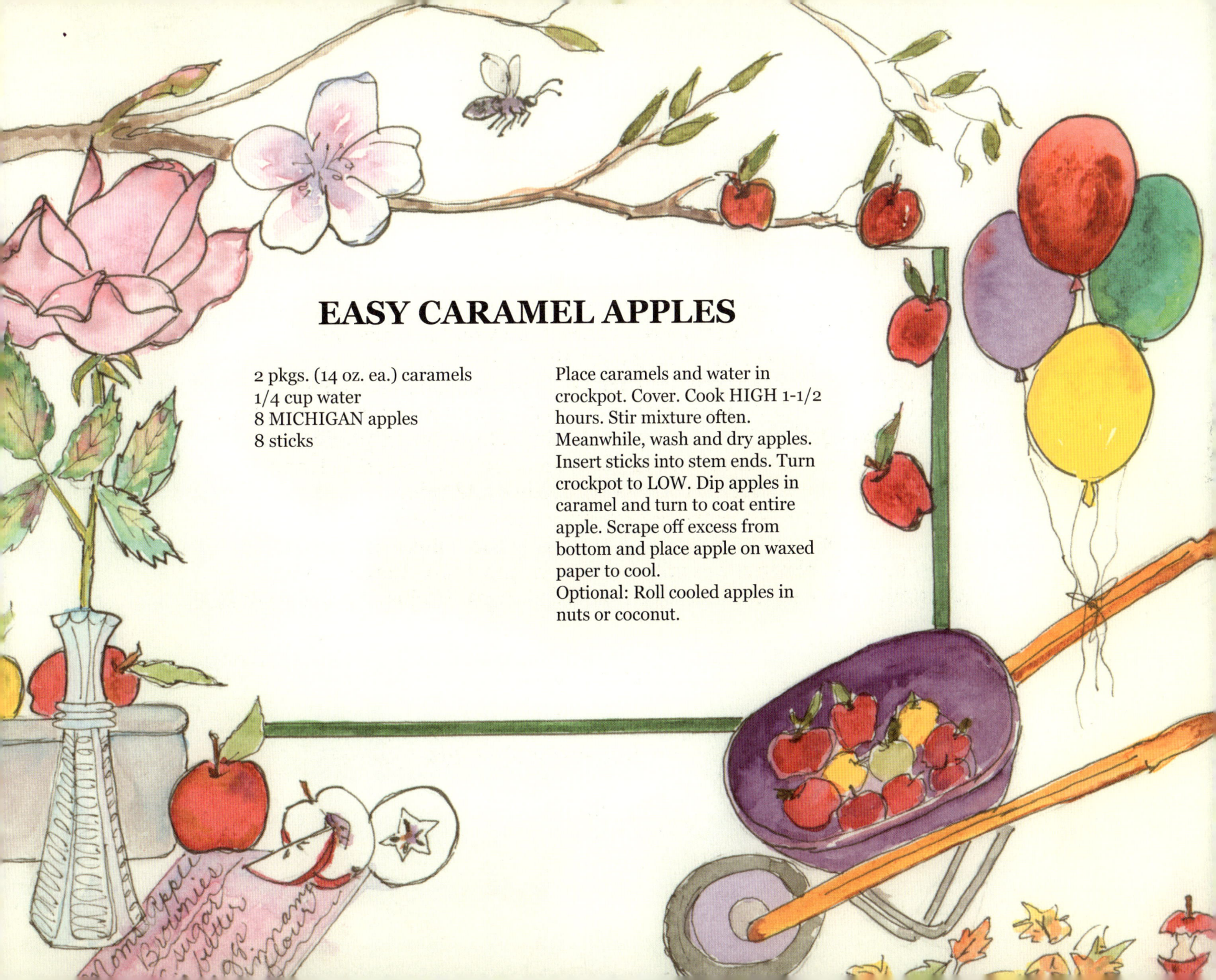

2 pkgs. (14 oz. ea.) caramels
1/4 cup water
8 MICHIGAN apples
8 sticks

Place caramels and water in crockpot. Cover. Cook HIGH 1-1/2 hours. Stir mixture often. Meanwhile, wash and dry apples. Insert sticks into stem ends. Turn crockpot to LOW. Dip apples in caramel and turn to coat entire apple. Scrape off excess from bottom and place apple on waxed paper to cool.
Optional: Roll cooled apples in nuts or coconut.

ANSWER KEY

p8-28 pies, p10-2000 pounds, p12-216 inches, p14-12 pounds, p16-6400 kernels, p18-30 minutes, p20-23 dozen, p22-14 weeks and 2 days, p24-2.3 pounds, p26-30,000 bushels, p28-360 calories, p30-432 apples, bk cover-50,400